THE POWER OF ONE WORD

THE POWER OF ONE WORD

TIM BOJKO

Copyright © 2025 by Tim Bojko
All rights reserved. No part of this book may be reproduced in any manner whatsoever without written permission except in the case of brief quotations embodied in critical articles and reviews.
First Printing, 2025

Contents

Dedication   vi
Acknowledgments   vii

    1   The Power of One Word as a Seed   1
    2   A Seed of Shame, The Vine of Lies   5
    3   When God Speaks Truth   10
    4   The War for Identity   17
    5   The Three P's to Prosperous Thinking   23
    6   Living as Ambassadors of Heaven   31

Starting a Relationship with Jesus   40

I dedicate this book to my Lord and Savior Jesus Christ, whose constant love and pursuit of me set me free and established me for His good work.

***

To my wife Corey whose wisdom, persistence, grace, tender love, and patience always amazes and inspires me. My heart completely trusts in her.

***

To my parents whose love, prayers, and example illustrated the continual grace and love of God through every situation. Thank you for faithfulness and obedience.

Acknowledgments

A heartfelt thank you to Troy Ledford, whose incredible cover art brought this book to life in ways words alone never could. His talent, creativity, and attention to detail have transformed the visual narrative and captured the very spirit of this story. To explore more of Troy's stunning work, please visit his portfolio at bluewhaleinnovation.com. You can contact him at tljledford@yahoo.com. Your artistry has set the perfect stage for my story—thank you for everything!

1

The Power of One Word as a Seed

Monday, August 23, 1982, was a warm and beautiful summer day in Northeastern Wisconsin. The breeze that swept through the trees carried more than fresh air - it carried promise. That morning, in a quiet corner of rural America surrounded by fields, creeks, and forest, I entered the world. My parents welcomed their second son on a day kissed by sunshine and simplicity.

Life in the country was everything a young boy with a wild imagination could hope for. We weren't distracted by city lights or screens. Instead, we had acres of land to roam, gardens to care for, and dirt beneath our fingernails. It was in this space of quiet wonder that something began to stir in me - something that, even then, I couldn't quite explain.

Curiosity. Creativity. Calling.

I remember running up and down the hills like I had wings on my feet. One moment I was a superhero, the next a world-famous explorer, discovering hidden treasure beneath pine trees or alongside the winding creek that cut through the land. The wind wasn't just wind - it was the voice of adventure. The rustling leaves weren't just noise - they were cues in a story I was living out in real time.

And I had a big imagination.

Give me a pile of LEGOs, and I would build cities, airports, vehicles, and bridges to nowhere. In the barn or by the garden, I would narrate epic journeys in my mind - some filled with danger, others full of discovery. I didn't need toys that talked or games that flashed. My thoughts were loud enough, vivid enough, and far-reaching enough to fill entire afternoons with wonder. And that wonder would grow into something else: vision.

What began as innocent play slowly took shape as a desire to create, to lead, to shape the world around me.

School brought new opportunities. I performed well in class, took on challenges with passion, and found joy in everything from science experiments to music practice. I had a natural drive, a hunger to figure things out - not just academically, but in life. What made people tick? What inspired them? What made something truly excellent? These questions buzzed in me even as a teenager.

In high school, I embraced both the arts and academics. I became drum major at my school. I played the flute - yes, the flute - and not just in band class. I studied it all the way through college, learning not only to play but to lead, to perform, to communicate with sound and presence. I chased goals. I aimed high. And I achieved a lot. By the time I graduated college, I held a 3.98 GPA and had earned respect in every setting I entered.

From the outside, things looked bright. On paper, I was thriving. I was stepping into leadership roles, being invited into rooms of influence, and getting early tastes of what it meant to shape outcomes and inspire others. But even with all the success, something quietly lingered underneath the surface.

There was a drive in me that wasn't fully rooted in passion - it was rooted in proving something. I couldn't quite explain it at the time. I just knew there was an unspoken voice in the background, always questioning my worth. No matter how high I climbed, it always asked, "Is it enough?"

And deeper still, behind the striving and the celebrating, behind the medals and the music, was a single word.

A word I never invited. A lie that came in unannounced.

A word that crept in before I knew how to guard my heart from lies.

A word that took root silently but began to shape everything.

That word was **ugly**.

* * *

PAUSE & REFLECT

What is one word you remember being spoken over you as a child?

How has it influenced your choices, relationships, or self-worth?

Do you see fruit in your life that might have grown from a painful root?

* * *

PRAYER DECLARATION

Father, reveal the words that have shaped me - both the life-giving and the limiting. Uproot every lie planted in my heart and begin preparing the soil of my soul for Your truth. I invite You to speak a new word over me today.

In Jesus' Name, Amen.

2

A Seed of Shame, The Vine of Lies

I was born with an eye condition that made my left pupil appear stuck. When people looked at me, especially children, it often invited laughter or worse - mockery. And while most of the remarks faded, the ones from girls cut the deepest. By middle school, I had already decided: *I hate girls. I will never marry a woman from Wisconsin.*

To my child-sized heart, Wisconsin was the whole world. And I'd made up my mind: keep your distance and protect your heart. But the damage had already been done. Repetition is how the enemy hides lies in plain sight, and the lie that formed in me was crystal clear:

I am ugly.

From there, the word multiplied. Ugly grew into *worthless*. Then *reclusive*. Then *unlovable, unholy, unworthy, no good,* and *failure*. A vine of lies had been planted in the soil of my heart - and it began to bear fruit.

No Good
Unlovable
Reclusive
Failure
Unworthy
Unholy
Worthless

UGLY

The vine of lies that were in my heart
Tim Bojko

That single word - ugly - became the root of a belief system — a vine of lies - that quietly controlled two critical areas of my life:

1. My Work Ethic.

I became addicted to results. Praise, performance, promotions - they weren't blessings, they were validation. Every medal I won, every raise I received was just another attempt to silence the lie screaming inside: *You're still not good enough.*

In America, we praise overwork and grind culture. We don't call it bondage - we call it hustle. But make no mistake, I was not a "high performer." I was a slave to achievement.

Then came a divine appointment.

While working at Northwestern Mutual and seeking a mentor to help me break into senior leadership, I reached out to several executive male leaders. One by one, they declined. Then a colleague asked, "Have you considered a female mentor?"

That suggestion rattled me. *A woman?* I wasn't sure how to even approach it, but after discussing it with my wife, we agreed I would reach out to Gina Tolzman, VP of Shared Operations at the time.

I expected another "no." Instead, Gina said yes.

I arrived at our first meeting like a corporate soldier - armed with binders, objectives, and a detailed plan. I was ready to prove my worth. But after sitting through my entire presentation, Gina smiled warmly and said:

> "Hi, I'm Gina Tolzman, and I know what your problem is - you're a results junkie."

Boom.

I was stunned. Everything I had achieved - everything I believed made me valuable - was reduced to a diagnosis I didn't want to hear. But she was right. I was working *from* pain, not *from* purpose. God would use her to begin unraveling the lies I had built my career on.

2. My Relationships.

The lies didn't just distort how I saw myself - they affected how I treated others. Especially the woman who would one day become my wife.

I met her in college. She was kind, beautiful, and strong. We had a natural friendship, but when the relationship turned toward romance, I pulled away - sabotaging connection to protect the wounded little boy inside me. I didn't believe I was lovable, so I made it impossible to be loved.

While I did the Christian things - reading Scripture, praying, serving - I kept God at arm's length. I didn't want Him getting too close to the part of me that still believed I was ugly and unworthy.

* * *

PAUSE & REFLECT

Have you ever struggled to believe that scripture personally applies to you?

What labels - spoken or unspoken - have rooted themselves in your heart?

Are there relationships in your life affected by your internal vine of lies?

Do you struggle with receiving what God says about you in the Bible?

* * *

SCRIPTURE MEDITATIONS

"Thou art all fair, my love; there is no spot in thee."

- Song of Solomon 4:7

"And be not conformed to this world: but be ye transformed by the renewing of your mind, that ye may prove what is that good, and acceptable, and perfect, will of God."

- Romans 12:2

"The thief cometh not, but for to steal, and to kill, and to destroy: I am come that they might have life, and that they might have it more abundantly."

- John 10:10

* * *

PRAYER DECLARATION

Lord, expose every root in my heart that was not planted by You. I break agreement with every word that contradicts Your truth. You say I am loved, chosen, and made in Your image. Uproot the lies, replant Your truth, and transform my inner world.

In Jesus' Name, Amen.

3

When God Speaks Truth

I didn't expect that morning to change my life. It started like many others - me, in my quiet time with the Lord, journal open, heart halfway in. You know the drill: read a chapter, pray a little, check the box. But that morning was different.

As I sat there flipping through scripture, my eyes landed on Psalm 18:19:"He brought me forth also into a large place; He was delivering me because He was pleased with me and delighted in me."

I paused.

I had read this before. Many times. But something about it caught me. And then-instinctively-I deflected.

"Well, that's about David," I muttered. "Of course You were pleased with him. He killed Goliath. He was king. A man after Your own heart. He earned it."

I kept reasoning, but heaven interrupted me.

Clear as day - sharper than anything I've ever heard in my spirit - God said:

"Who told you I'm not pleased with you?"

I froze.

His words cut through me - not to wound, but to heal. That single sentence exposed the quiet shame I had carried for decades. I didn't believe God delighted in me. I believed He tolerated me. Used me maybe. But delighted in me? No way.

But in that moment, everything shifted.

The Father's Lap.

I don't know how else to explain it - except to say I felt wrapped. Like God Himself lifted me into His lap and pulled me close. Not because I had done something remarkable. Not because I earned a moment of intimacy. But simply because I was His.

I wept.

I saw something I had never seen before: I wasn't just God's servant - I was His son. And not just any son - a son who delighted the heart of His Father. A son who He saw through Jesus. Made righteous. Holy. Pure. Not because of my works, but because of what Jesus did.

That truth broke chains I didn't even know I still carried. Chains of performance. Of striving. Of deep-down unworthiness masked by achievement. All of it began to unravel.

It was time to let go of the masks.

Up to that point in my life, I had succeeded by striving. State championships. Drum major. Fortune 100 accolades. Innovation awards. It all looked shiny on the outside. But deep down, I was still trying to prove I wasn't the ugly little boy with a patch on his eye.

I wore the mask well. But masks don't breathe.

I had never let God into the parts of me I tried to hide - not really. I gave Him access to the "church" version of me. The polished version. The good boy who memorized scripture and tithed and checked all the spiritual boxes.

But God didn't want a cleaned-up visitor. He wanted me - raw, real, vulnerable. And it was in that moment, crumpled in His love, that I finally *fully* surrendered. I was all in.

I fully surrendered to His Voice.

"Lord," I whispered, "if You really are this good... if You really delight in me... then take it all. My fear. My shame. My striving. My performance. My pride. Even the pain that's strangely become familiar."

And I'll never forget what He said next:

"I will. But I want to do more than that. I want to replace it with something better – TRUTH!"

He showed me the vine of lies I had allowed to grow in my heart. Words like *ugly, unworthy, unlovable, not enough.* They had choked out the **truth**.

But God didn't just pull out the weeds. He planted something new.

A single word: **Lovely**.

He spoke it like a seed. And from that seed grew a new vine: *Beautiful. Holy. Worthy. Precious. Beloved.* A vine of truth. A vine rooted not in my performance, but in my position as His child.

And then... worship flowed.

Vine of Truth about who God says I am in my heart
Tim Bojko

Not the kind with lights or lyrics or hands raised because everyone else was. But the worship of a heart completely undone. A heart that had nothing left to prove and everything to receive.

That was the day I understood that worship is not a song - it's a surrender. A love response to love received. A heart positioned to adore the awe of God forever. A heart that found sweet intimacy that nothing else could ever compare to.

I wasn't singing to get closer to God. I was singing because I finally realized He was already in me. He wasn't waiting in some holy tabernacle - I am the tabernacle. And when I worshiped, heaven sang back.

Scripture became alive in me:
"The Lord your God is in your midst... He will rejoice over you with singing." (Zeph. 3:17)

Yes - He rejoices over me (and you too!).

I had spent years believing the lie that God was disappointed in me. That He expected more. That I hadn't measured up. But that morning crushed those lies. Not with condemnation, but with compassion.

Romans 8:1 came alive like never before:

"There is therefore now no condemnation for those who are in Christ Jesus."

None.

Not even a trace. Not for the shame I buried, the mistakes I made, or the striving I called ambition. He didn't just forgive me. **He embraced me.**

Since that day, my relationship with God hasn't been about tasks - it's been about togetherness.

I journal now - not because I have to, but because I want to remember every word He speaks to me. I sit with Him - not just for answers, but for affection. I listen - not only to get instruction, but to experience His voice rejoicing over me.

And when the old lies whisper again (because they try), I don't entertain them. I go back to the vine. I go back to the lap of my Father. I worship. I surrender again.

Because this walk? It's not about being impressive. It's about being *intimate*.

* * *

PAUSE & REFLECT

When was the last time you asked God how He thinks about you?

Do you believe He delights in you - even in your brokenness?

What areas of your life have been fueled by striving instead of intimate relationship with Jesus?

* * *

SCRIPTURE MEDITATIONS

"The LORD thy God in the midst of thee is mighty; He will save, He will rejoice over thee with joy; He will rest in his love, He will joy over thee with singing."

- Zephaniah 3:17

"Behold, what manner of love the Father hath bestowed upon us, that we should be called the sons of God: therefore the world knoweth us not, because it knew him not."

- 1 John 3:1

"For we are his workmanship, created in Christ Jesus unto good works, which God hath before ordained that we should walk in them."

- Ephesians 2:10

* * *

PRAYER DECLARATION

Father, I renounce the lie that I must earn Your love or approval. Thank You that You are pleased with me not because of what I do, but because of who I am in Christ. Help me live as a son, not a servant. Let my identity be rooted in delight, not performance.

In Jesus' Name, Amen.

4

The War for Identity

Looking back, I can trace so many of my internal battles - whether emotional, spiritual, or even professional - down to a single root: identity.

I didn't always have the language for it. For a long time, I just thought I had to try harder. Push more. Be better. But underneath the striving, perfectionism, and occasional burnout was one core issue:

I didn't truly believe I was enough.

That belief didn't come from nowhere. It was planted early. Maybe you can relate. Satan is strategic to plant seeds of lies early in an attempt to disrupt us from God's goodness and His plans. Thankfully, God is faithful and always pursuing us to reveal His truth!

Let's be clear about something important - Satan doesn't attack haphazardly-he is strategic. His aim is clear, consistent, and calculated. Just like in Eden, when he asked Eve, *"Did God really say...?"*, his goal wasn't just to deceive - it was to **separate**.

That's what the enemy wants: to separate us from the love of Christ.

Because he knows if he can get us to question God's heart, we'll drift from His truth. And once we feel separated from love, identity begins to crumble.

That's the cycle:

Steal. Kill. Destroy.

Steal your identity.

Kill your value.

Destroy your purpose.

(John 10:10)

But the moment the enemy gets you to question God's love for you, the downward spiral begins.

He can't actually separate you from the love of Christ - Romans 8:38–39 makes that abundantly clear. But if he can convince you that you've been separated, that God is distant or disappointed, then he doesn't have to take your purpose - **you'll abandon it yourself.**

Because when you stop believing you're loved, you start living like you're not.

And when you live unloved, everything begins to unravel - your confidence, your identity, your relationships, even your sense of calling.

That's why Jesus came - not just to forgive sin, but to restore **abundant life** (John 10:10).

And that life begins with love.

Love is what builds connection.

Connection forms belonging.

And belonging lays the foundation for our identity in Christ.

Jesus didn't just talk about your value - **He demonstrated it.**

His sacrifice was the ultimate declaration:

"You are worth dying for."

When we receive that love, we stop chasing worth - and start living from it.

That's what leads to purpose. That's what gives rise to faith, sustains hope, and ultimately brings lasting fulfillment.

Love First. Then Purpose.

That's the difference between the world's way and God's way. The world says, "Perform, then you'll be accepted." God says, "You're accepted - now come walk in your purpose."

His order is:

He restores identity: *"You are My child."*

He reveals value: *"You are precious in My sight."*

He releases purpose: *"I've appointed you for such a time as this."*

Everything begins with love. Not effort. Not credentials. Not perfection.

Love.

It changed *everything.*

That shift didn't just heal me - it changed the way I loved others.

As a husband, I began to lead from security instead of insecurity. My wife didn't just get a provider - she got a partner. A man anchored in God's love.

As a father, I started to see how critical it is for my daughters to grow up with a dad who knows who he is. Not just in role - but in identity. They don't need me to be flawless. They need me to be free.

Even as a leader, I stopped chasing affirmation and started leading from overflow. I no longer needed success to validate me. God already had.

A Word for You.

If you've been living under a label that God never wrote - if the enemy has whispered lies that have shaped how you see yourself - it's time to let the truth speak louder.

You don't need to become someone else.

You need to become who God says you already are. It starts with asking Jesus to create a new heart in you - one that is holy, pure, and righteous.

So let Him in. Let Him uproot the vine of lies. Let Him speak a new word over you - one that heals, anchors, and launches you into His eternal purpose.

Because when you know you are loved, you stop performing and start becoming.

You don't work for identity - you live from it.

And that's when everything changes.

John 8:36 states *"If the Son therefore shall make you free, ye shall be free indeed."*

You are free! Free from guilt, sin, shame, condemnation, wrath, and the lies from Satan. Go in the freedom of who Jesus created you to be.

* * *

PAUSE & REFLECT

Where do you see Satan trying to twist your identity?

What lies of Satan are you believing?

What lies about God are you believing?

Do you base your value on what you do or who you are in Christ?

What truth does God say about you?

* * *

SCRIPTURE MEDITATIONS

"But ye are a chosen generation, a royal priesthood, an holy nation, a peculiar people; that ye should shew forth the praises of him who hath called you out of darkness into his marvelous light:"

- 1 Peter 2:9

"The Spirit itself beareth witness with our spirit, that we are the children of God:"

- Romans 8:16

"Before I formed thee in the belly I knew thee; and before thou camest forth out of the womb I sanctified thee, and I ordained thee a prophet unto the nations."

- Jeremiah 1:5

* * *

PRAYER DECLARATION

Father, I declare that I am who You say I am. I break agreement with every lie spoken over my identity. I am Your child, chosen and loved. My value is not earned; it's bestowed by You. Restore my sense of purpose and position me in the fullness of who You created me to be.

In Jesus' Name, Amen.

5

The Three P's to Prosperous Thinking

"*Beloved, I wish above all things that thou mayest prosper and be in health, even as thy soul (mind) prospereth.*" - 3 John 1:2

God gave me a framework to cast down imaginations and break strongholds in the thought life. I call it the **Three P's to Prosperous Thinking:**

1. Purpose Thoughts

2. Position Thoughts

3. Power Thoughts

Each one is a truth anchor for your identity and destiny. When applied daily, they shape how you think, live, lead, and love. This is not self-help - it's Spirit-led renewal.

Purpose Thoughts: Vision That Comes from God.

Purpose thoughts are focused on heaven's assignment for your life. They give direction, motivation, and endurance when opposition rises.

One of my core purpose thoughts is this:

"Billionaire Bojko blessing billions of people."

It's not about finances - it's about **impact**. That phrase was written on the whiteboard of my soul by the Holy Spirit. It speaks to my God-given mission to inspire and nurture others to fulfill their eternal purpose.

But even if you don't yet have a specific or personalized vision, you already carry heaven's general mission:

The Great Commission.

"Go ye therefore, and teach all nations, baptizing them in the Name of the Father, and of the Son, and of the Holy Ghost: Teaching them to observe all things..."

- Matthew 28:19–20

"Who will have all men to be saved, and to come unto the knowledge of the truth."

- 1 Timothy 2:4

That means your life already has purpose. Whether you're a stay-at-home parent, a CEO, a student, or a janitor - your daily walk can participate in the mission of Christ: to love, reach, teach, and transform lives for eternity.

Even Jesus declared His own purpose:

> "*He that committeth sin is of the devil; for the devil sinneth from the beginning. For this purpose the Son of God was manifested, that he might destroy the works of the devil.*"
>
> - 1 John 3:8

Nehemiah rebuilt the walls of Jerusalem with laser focus despite sabotage and mockery. He declared, "*I am doing a great work, so that I cannot come down*" (Nehemiah 6:3). That's a purpose thought in action.

Position Thoughts: Who You Are in Christ.

Position thoughts are rooted in identity - not in performance. They keep you from striving and start you walking in intimate relationship with Jesus.

Before I understood my position, I lived under the weight of the word **ugly**. That lie grew into a vine of false beliefs: worthless, unholy, unlovable. But one encounter with God changed everything. He asked me:

"Who told you I do not delight in you?"

That question broke the lie. God replaced *ugly* with **lovely**. That one word became the seed of a new vine: precious, worthy, beautiful, holy, and beloved.

"But ye are a chosen generation, a royal priesthood, an holy nation, a peculiar people…"

- 1 Peter 2:9

"As He is, so are we in this world."

- 1 John 4:17

Gideon saw himself as the weakest of the weak. But God called him a "mighty man of valor" (Judges 6:12). Heaven sees differently. Identity comes before behavior. Your position determines your fruit.

Power Thoughts: Strength from the Source.

Power thoughts are rooted in your divine supply - God Himself.

In corporate life, I once had to approach an executive known for saying "no" to everything. But I had learned to speak power thoughts over myself:

- God made me able.
- I am an overcomer.
- His favor surrounds me.
- His joy gives me strength.

That meeting didn't just lead to approval - it opened a door for emotional healing in the executive's life. That's what happens when you walk in authority born from truth.

"I can do all things through Christ who strengthens me." - Philippians 4:13

"Not by might, nor by power, but by My Spirit..." - Zechariah 4:6

"The joy of the Lord is your strength." - Nehemiah 8:10

David didn't trust Saul's armor - he trusted God. He declared:

"Thou comest to me with a sword, and with a spear,... but I come to thee in the Name of the LORD of hosts..." - 1 Samuel 17:45

Power thoughts speak victory before it manifests.

The Fruit of Prosperous Thinking.

When Purpose, Position, and Power thoughts become your daily mindset, the results are undeniable:

- Confidence in your calling
- Clarity in direction
- Peace in pressure
- Boldness in influence
- Joy in everyday life

This is how Jesus lived. This is how the early church shook the world. This is how your soul prospers - and your life follows.

"A good man out of the good treasure of his heart bringeth forth that which is good;... for of the abundance of the heart his mouth speaketh."

- Luke 6:45

"be ye transformed by the renewing of your mind,..."

- Romans 12:2

* * *

PAUSE AND REFLECT

What purpose word or vision has God spoken over your life?

Are you living in your true identity - or still striving for acceptance?

Where do you need to exchange fear-based thoughts for Spirit birthed revelation based declarations?

Which of the 3 P's do you most need to strengthen today?

* * *

SCRIPTURE MEDITATIONS

"Beloved, I wish above all things that thou mayest prosper and be in health, even as thy soul prospereth."

- 3 John 1:2

"Behold, I will bring it health and cure, and I will cure them, and will reveal unto them the abundance of peace and truth."

- Jeremiah 33:6

"Go ye therefore, and teach all nations, baptizing them in the name of the Father, and of the Son, and of the Holy Ghost: Teaching them to observe all things whatsoever I have commanded you: and, lo, I am with you always, even unto the end of the world. Amen."

- Matthew 28: 19-20

"But ye are a chosen generation, a royal priesthood, an holy nation, a peculiar people; that ye should shew forth the praises of him who hath called you out of darkness into his marvelous light:"

- 1 Peter 2:9

"I can do all things through Christ which strengtheneth me."

- Philippians 4:13

"And be not conformed to this world: but be ye transformed by the renewing of your mind, that ye may prove what is that good, and acceptable, and perfect, will of God."

- Romans 12:2

"And I sent messengers unto them, saying, I am doing a great work, so that I cannot come down: why should the work cease, whilst I leave it, and come down to you?"

- Nehemiah 6:3

* * *

PRAYER DECLARATION

Father, I surrender my thought life to You. I reject the lies of the enemy and receive Your truth. Thank You that I am called with purpose, positioned with identity, and filled with Your power.

I declare:

- I am a kingdom-minded visionary
- I am chosen, holy, and dearly loved
- I am empowered by the Spirit to overcome
- I walk in joy, favor, and divine strength
- I prosper as my soul prospers

Let my thoughts reflect heaven. Let my words echo eternity. Let my life produce fruit that remains.

In Jesus' Name, Amen.

6

Living as Ambassadors of Heaven

"*Now then we are ambassadors for Christ, as though God did beseech you by us:*"

- 2 Corinthians 5:20

We were never created to live in survival mode. From the beginning, we were designed for intimate communion with God, to walk in the cool of the day with Him, and from that place of love and identity, carry out His purposes on the earth. As sons and daughters, we carry the DNA of our Father. As ambassadors, we represent His heart, His kingdom, and His power in every space we occupy.

In earlier chapters, I shared how a single word, *ugly*, had once shaped my entire self-image. It grew into a vine of lies that governed my behavior, relationships, and leadership style. Even though I was saved, went to church, and had outward success, I was not living in the fullness of my identity. It wasn't until God asked me, "*Who told you I do not delight in you?*" that the truth began to replace the lies. That truth - that I am *lovely, valuable, holy, precious, worthy* - didn't just restore my soul. It began to change how I lived, worked, loved, and led.

That transformation is not just about freedom for me. It's about assignment. We are not just rescued sons; we are sent ones. Wherever we go - our businesses, homes, meetings, cars, or communities - we are ambassadors of heaven. The Holy Spirit doesn't just live *in* us. He flows *through* us. Every space we enter becomes an embassy of heaven.

When you know who you are and whose you are, your very presence changes atmospheres. You bring light into darkness, peace into chaos, healing into brokenness. Your life becomes a continual overflow of the love, joy, power, and compassion of Jesus.

Intimacy Fuels Ambassadorship.

Intimacy with God is where this lifestyle begins. This isn't about religious routines. It's about walking with the Father, listening to His voice, and receiving His love daily. Before Jesus performed miracles or called disciples, He was affirmed by His Father: *"This is My beloved Son, in whom I am well pleased"* (Matthew 3:17). His ministry flowed from identity, and His identity was forged in intimacy.

We must abide in that same place. Intimacy reminds us that we don't minister for approval, but from acceptance. When we spend time in His presence, we are filled with the very attributes of heaven: righteousness, peace, joy, and wisdom.

> *"Abide in me, and I in you. As the branch cannot bear fruit of itself, except it abide in the vine; no more can ye, except ye abide in me."*

\- John 15:4

> *"The Lord GOD hath given me the tongue of the learned, that I should know how to speak a word in season to him that is weary: he wakeneth morning by morning, he wakeneth mine ear to hear as the learned."*

\- Isaiah 50:4

From Inner Victory to Outward Overflow.

When I began replacing lies with truth, my thoughts shifted. So did my behavior. My relationship with my wife grew in grace. My leadership changed from striving to stewardship. My corporate success no longer came at the cost of my soul. This is what it means to live from victory rather than for it.

> *"But thanks be to God, which giveth us the victory through our Lord Jesus Christ."*

\- 1 Corinthians 15:57

The world doesn't need more Christians who are merely surviving. It needs sons and daughters who know they are seated in heavenly places (Ephesians 2:6), walking in righteousness (2 Corinthians 5:21), filled with divine power (Acts 1:8), and flowing in unshakable peace (Philippians 4:7).

And this is the link back to the **Power of One Word**:

it took one false word to bind me, but it also took one true word to free me. That is the miracle of intimacy. It doesn't take a sermon. It takes a whisper. When God speaks one word into your identity - lovely, chosen, clean, mine - it can dismantle decades of satanic lies. And that same voice now flows through you.

Every Space You Occupy is Sacred.

The realization that we are temples of the Holy Spirit (1 Corinthians 6:19) changes how we view everything. My desk isn't just a desk. It's an embassy. My car is not just transportation - it's a sanctuary. Whether I'm in a boardroom or a grocery store, I carry the presence of God.

As ambassadors, we bring heaven to earth. In business, this means we speak with integrity, solve problems with God-given wisdom, and love our coworkers with supernatural compassion. In our homes, we cultivate peace and joy. On the streets, we carry healing and hope.

I've seen it firsthand-from praying for strangers at conferences to speaking a word of knowledge over someone in a restaurant. These aren't platform moments. They're overflow moments. And they are available to every believer.

> "He that believeth on me, as the scripture hath said, out of his belly shall flow rivers of living water."
>
> - John 7:38

Overflow Transforms Culture.

You were never meant to contain the Spirit. You were meant to *release* Him. Revival doesn't begin on platforms. It begins in surrendered hearts. It flows from dining tables, office chairs, and hospital rooms.

When you walk in love, joy, peace, and compassion, you carry the culture of heaven.

> "For the kingdom of God is not meat and drink; but righteousness, and peace, and joy in the Holy Ghost."
>
> - Romans 14:17

This is how nations are changed: one whisper in the quiet, one act of obedience, one look of compassion, one word of encouragement, one prayer in a hallway, one generous act in secret. **Intimacy births overflow, and overflow births transformational revival.**

The early church didn't have social media, stages, or status. Yet they turned cities upside down (Acts 17:6). Why? Because they were full of God's Spirit and unashamed of His message. That same Spirit lives in you. And the world is still waiting for sons and daughters to rise.

The Call to Transform Nations.

Isaiah prophesied, *"Of the increase of His government and peace there shall be no end"* (Isaiah 9:7). God's government is expanding, not retreating. And He's using ordinary people like you and me to do it.

Whether you lead a business or sweep floors, disciple your children or preach to thousands, you are an ambassador of heaven. You are a carrier of divine strategy, love, and power. Don't wait for a microphone. Release what God has placed in you now. It is enough to shift cultures, rebuild families, and disciple nations.

The same Satanic thoughts that once held you in bondage are binding others right now. But your intimacy and obedience can be the catalyst that frees them. What once enslaved you has now equipped you to set captives free. That is the power of one word released in the love of God. It is now our time. Let us receive and rise up in the fullness of Love & Truth that He made us to be. As we have received, freely give to everyone around you. The world is hurting because they are all bound by lies. It is time to go and set them free. Glory to God!

* * *

PAUSE AND REFLECT

Are you living as a child of God or a servant of fear?

What is blocking you from living in overflow?

Who around you might still be bound by the same lies God has set you free from?

What would shift in your life if you fully believed your everyday moments carry Kingdom impact?

How can you practically bring the atmosphere of heaven into your workplace, home, or car this week?

* * *

SCRIPTURE MEDITATIONS

"Now then we are ambassadors for Christ, as though God did beseech you by us: we pray you in Christ's stead, be ye reconciled to God."

- 2 Corinthians 5:20

"Abide in me, and I in you. As the branch cannot bear fruit of itself, except it abide in the vine; no more can ye, except ye abide in me. I am the vine, ye are the branches: He that abideth in me, and I in him, the same bringeth forth much fruit: for without me ye can do nothing"

- John 15:4-5

"For the kingdom of God is not meat and drink; but righteousness, and peace, and joy in the Holy Ghost."

- Romans 14:17

"And hath raised us up together, and made us sit together in heavenly places in Christ Jesus"

- Ephesians 2:6

"Of the increase of his government and peace there shall be no end, upon the throne of David, and upon his kingdom, to order it, and to establish it with judgment and with justice from henceforth even for ever. The zeal of the LORD of hosts will perform this."

- Isaiah 9:7

"What? know ye not that your body is the temple of the Holy Ghost which is in you, which ye have of God, and ye are not your own?"

- 1 Corinthians 6:19

"He that believeth on me, as the scripture hath said, out of his belly shall flow rivers of living water."

- John 7:38

"The Spirit of the Lord is upon me, because he hath anointed me to preach the gospel to the poor; he hath sent me to heal the brokenhearted, to preach deliverance to the captives, and recovering of sight to the blind, to set at liberty them that are bruised, to preach the acceptable year of the Lord."

- Luke 4:18-19

* * *

PRAYER DECLARATION

Father, Thank You for choosing me to be both Your child and Your ambassador. Thank You that Your Spirit lives in me and flows through me. Today, I align my life with Your heart. I surrender my fears, my spaces, and my influence to You.

I declare:

- I am loved, chosen, and sent.

- I carry the atmosphere of heaven into every room.

- My thoughts, words, and actions reflect Your Kingdom.

- I live from the truth of Your Word, not the lies of the enemy.

- I move in compassion, power, and boldness.

What You did in me, You will do through me - for others to be set free.

Use my life to bring light to darkness, peace to storms, and freedom to those still trapped in the lies I once believed. Let one word spoken in love be the seed of transformation for families, businesses, and even nations.

In Jesus' Name, Amen.

Starting a Relationship with Jesus

Today you read my story of how Jesus restored my identity and relationship with Him. God loves you so much that He does not want anyone to live without an intimate relationship with Him. It is because of that relationship that I know with confidence I will be in heaven when I die. But His gift isn't just about eternity—it's about the overwhelming joy, peace, and purpose that fills your life here and now when you accept Him. The same love that secures your future in heaven transforms your present. Do you know where you will be when you die? Make the quality decision today to make Him Lord over your life, for the plans He has for you are far greater than anything you can imagine. His saving grace forgives and cleanses us so that we can begin the journey of walking daily with God—loved, restored, and free. He meets you right where you are—not in perfection, but in surrender. You were not made to live entangled in lies, fear, or shame. You were made to live loved.

You don't have to carry the labels the world has put on you. Jesus came to exchange every lie for truth—every word like "ugly," "unworthy," or "forgotten" for His words: "lovely," "valuable," "chosen," and "redeemed." The same God who transformed my life wants to do the same for you. This is not just inspiration—this is invitation. A single word from Him can break every chain. A single "yes" from you can change your life forever.

If you're ready to step into a new life—full of peace, purpose, and identity in Christ—say this prayer from your heart.

* * *

Dear Heavenly Father,

I come before you, knowing that I am a sinner and I am asking that you forgive me from my sins. Create in me a new heart and I accept and receive and make Jesus the Lord of my life. I surrender all my life to Him. Jesus thank you for coming into my heart and making me new. Father, I know that Your Word says I'm saved when I confess it and I know now that I am saved. I am a child of God.

Thank you, Lord Jesus!

Glory to God!

* * *

www.ingramcontent.com/pod-product-compliance
Lightning Source LLC
Chambersburg PA
CBHW050046080526
44586CB00014B/1486